WALKING CL

CW00418605

GREAT OUSE n

Number Fifteen in the popular series of
walking guides

ontents

/alked, Written and Drawn by Clive Brown

Clive Brown 2003 – 2015

blished by Clive Brown
BN 978-1-907669-15-6

PLEASE
Take care of the countryside
Your leisure is someone's livelihood

Close gates
Start no fires
Keep away from livestock and animals
Do not stray from marked paths
Take litter home
Do not damage walls, hedgerows or fences
Cross only at stiles or gates
Protect plants, trees and wildlife
Keep dogs on leads
Respect crops, machinery and rural property
Do not contaminate water

Although not essential we recommend good walking boots; during hot weather take something to drink on the way. All walks can easily be negotiated by an averagely fit person. The routes have been recently walked and surveyed, changes can however occur, please follow any signed diversions. Some paths cross fields which are under cultivation. All distances and times are approximate.

The maps give an accurate portrayal of the area, but scale has however been sacrificed in some cases for the sake of clarity and to fit restrictions of page size.

Walking Close To have taken every care in the research and production of this guide but cannot be held responsible for the safety of anyone using them.

During very wet weather, parts of these walks may become impassable through flooding, check before starting out. Stiles and rights of way can get overgrown during the summer; folding secateurs are a useful addition to a walker's rucksack.

Thanks to Angela for help in production of these booklets

Views or comments?
walkingcloseto@yahoo.co.uk

Reproduced from Ordnance Survey Mapping on behalf of The Controller of Her Majesty's Stationery Office.   © Crown Copyright License No. 100037980.

Walking Close To the Great Ouse
near Bedford

he walks contained in this booklet make use of rights of way, national recreational aths and riverside paths in the area northwest of Bedford. There is very little alking on roads except where unavoidable. Most are on firm, good quality paths nd well marked and signposted. Paths may cross fields under cultivation and some re more obscure and less well directed; the detailed instructions will guide past ese points. Some of the walks are in areas popular with walkers already; others re in areas less popular and perhaps less accessible.

arrow medieval bridges are still used at Bromham, Oakley and Harrold setting the cene for the far less frenetic pace of the country roads in the area between the usy A6 and A428 covered by this booklet.

he county town of Bedford is probably best known for its connection with John unyan (1628-1688), the author of 'Pilgrim's Progress'; he was born in nearby lstow but lived in Bedford from 1655. He served in the parliamentary army during e Civil War before becoming a fervent Baptist. Between 1660 and 1672 he was nprisoned in Bedford jail for unlicensed preaching. 'Pilgrim's Progress' was written uring his second term of imprisonment in 1676/7.

series of disused gravel pits attract a variety of wildfowl and water mammals; eep a look out for otters! Several pits have been designated nature reserves; the arrold-Odell Country Park between the two villages is a particularly fruitful area to bserve all forms of wildlife.

ufted Duck are widespread in the Ouse Valley; it is now one of Britain's most ommon ducks. The species never bred here before Victorian times but now there re around ten thousand residents and a half a million summer visitors.

Je feel that it would be difficult to get lost with the instructions and map in this ooklet, but recommend carrying an Ordnance Survey map. The walks are on xplorer Maps Nos 207 and 224; Landranger No. 153 covers at a smaller scale. oads, geographical features and buildings, not on our map but visible from the alk can be easily identified

1   Sharnbrook Tunnel

6 Miles   3 Hours

Find a parking space in Souldrop off the A6 south of Rushden. No toilets, local pub the 'Bedford Arms'.

1   Start from the village green, head down the slope into Back Lane, keep directio
past the green triangle and over the railway bridge. Continue uphill on the tarmac bridleway; follow it to the right then left through a gate and straight on to a crossroads at a 'Give Way' sign. Carry on ahead, turn left with the road at a marke
post and keep going past New Farm to a T-junction between farm buildings and Barwick Spinney on the right.

2   Turn right down the stony bridleway past the spinney and Barwick Wood; go right for a few yards then continue original direction with the dyke and Brownage Wood to the left. Walk up to the perimeter of Santa Pod Raceway, turn right then left around it, turn right again at the corner and then left through a hedge gap.

3   Turn right, facing away from Santa Pod, walk between Great Hayes Wood on the left and the hedge to the right along Forty Foot Lane, a distinct track. After three quarters of a mile go over the railway bridge and the top of Sharnbrook Tunnel. Continue through a gate onto a more substantial bridleway; keep straight on along a rutted grass track signposted Three Shires Way, as this bridleway swing
right and walk up to the A6 road.

4   Cross slightly right, still signposted Three Shires Way, go along the left hand side of the field and turn right at the corner. At the next corner cross the sleeper bridge and walk to the left around the edge of the wood eventually reaching two marker posts. Bear left through a wide hedge gap.

5   Go over the field, which may be under cultivation but a track should be visible within any crop, heading just to the right of Knotting church. Turn right along the field edge with the hedge to the left, keep along this field edge as the Three Shires Way goes left. Carry on bearing right in a dip between the fields back to the wood.

6   Continue down the wide bridleway between Sheeprack and West Wood, bearing slightly right to the road and walk across.

7   Take the footpath just to the right, walk across the scrubland, through the hedge gap to the left and over the sleeper footbridge. Cross the field in the arrowed direction, a track should be visible, over the stile and go along the right hand side of the field between the stable and the conifers. Cross the stile and keep direction through the gate down the enclosed path into Souldrop and your vehicle.

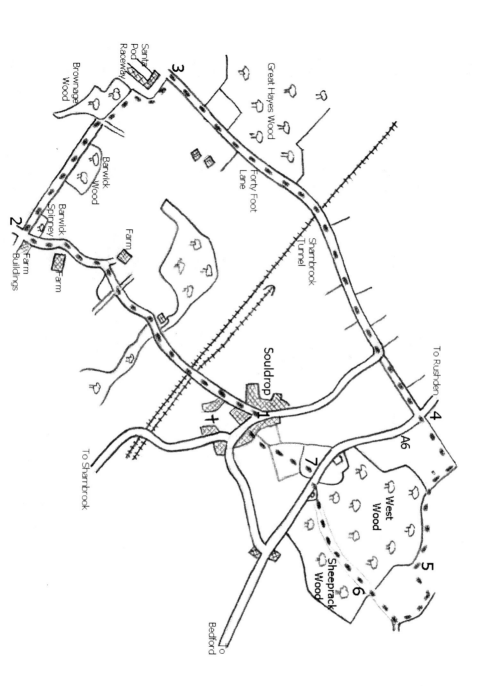

Santa Pod Raceway
Brownage Wood
Barwick Wood
Barwick Spinney
Farm Buildings
Farm
Farm
Great Hayes Wood
Forty Foot Lane
Shambrook Tunnel
To Rushden
To Shambrook
Souldrop
A6
West Wood
Sheeprack Wood
Bedford

3
2
4
5
6
7
1

2   Great Ouse Horseshoe

6 Miles $2^1/_2$ Hours

Find a parking space in Pavenham, no toilets.

1   Start from the footpath opposite Weavers Lane. Go down the footpath and turn right at the end, follow the field edge round to the corner and cross a stile by a long thatched cottage; go past the cottage to the road and turn left at the signpost. Go through the kissing gate and down the path curving to the right; cross the stile and continue on the path between trees and over the next stile keeping the hedge to the right. Cross the sleeper footbridge/stile into the riverside meadow.

2   Walk closer to the river as it starts to go left past a marker post and over a boardwalk and a metal railed footbridge. In this field follow a noticeable track to the right of the trees ahead past marker posts and through the kissing gate. Go down the fenced track and bear left at the end through another kissing gate.

3   Turn left over the stile at the end of the trees (Wood Craft) then right over a tiny footbridge and down a hedge lined path, cross a stile then turn left cross another stile and continue along the left hand side of the field. (Signs here are a little confusing). Turn right at the corner, still following the fence; turn left at the next stile and right on the other side to continue the original direction with the hedge now on the right. Go over another stile, through two gates in the corner and the kissing gate under the church.

4   Follow the wall then bear right up the slope into Stevington. At a signpost on the left go through the kissing gate and take a right hand diagonal to another kissing gate. Cross the footbridge and bear left alongside the stream at the backs of the houses, continue over the next footbridge turn right with the stream to the right carry on up to the road and turn left.

5   Walk along to Stevington Belt, a line of trees on the left stretching down to the river. Go down to the river with the trees on the left and turn right. Follow the riverbank all the way to the bridges at Oakley (keep to the right of the island).

6   Turn left over the bridges, as the road turns right go straight on up the obvious track at the sign and through the enclosed path onto the road in Oakley. Turn left and walk along the roadside path to the corner turn right past the 'Bedford Arms' to the main road by the Oakley sign and turn left.

7   Cross the bridge over the river and turn left along the permissive path over two stiles and follow the riverbank to the corner of the wood furthest away from the river. Turn right then left twice keeping to the edge of this enormous field, turn right at the end corner alongside the narrow belt of trees.

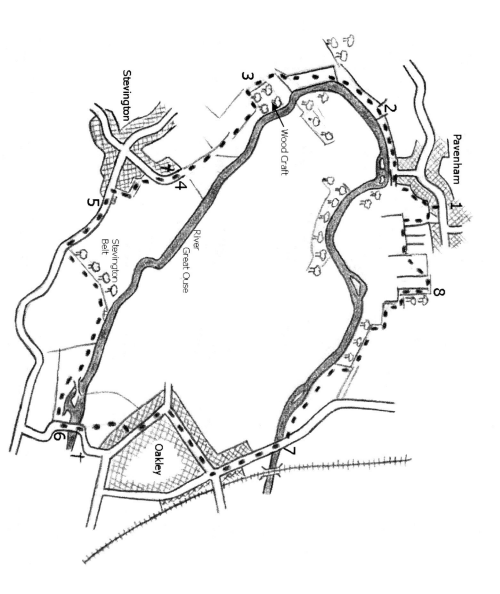

Turn left over a stile at the signpost; over the next stile take a left hand diagonal to a stile marked by a signpost on the other side, cross and continue on the right hand field edge. Bear right at the marker post and stile before the end and go up the right hand edge of this field. Turn left at the end and then right along the footpath used on the outward leg, into Pavenham and your vehicle.

5:E

3   Yelnow Lane

$6^1/_2$ Miles   3 Hours

Park in the Harrold-Odell Country Park near the Visitor Centre in Harrold. Toilets, café and shop on site.

1   Walk away from the car park on the wide hardcore path between the lakes and go all the way into Odell. Continue past the 'Bell' and the Odell sign and walk up the slope with the stone wall to the right. Turn left on the far side of the church up Church Lane.

2   Turn right over the stile at the footpath sign, keep direction over the stile on the right and carry on across two more stiles. Follow the path between fence and hedge past two yellow topped posts and go straight on over the next field; this field may be under cultivation but a track should be well marked within any crop.

3   Cross the sleeper footbridge and take a slight left hand diagonal to a yellow topped post in the distant corner (a track should be visible). Cross this footbridge and turn right along the right hand field edge, at the next marker post go diagonally to the top left hand corner and turn left down the edge of the wood.

4   Bear left in the corner along the byway Yelnow Lane and keep going around several bends and past marker posts to a concrete standing at a plant/works area.

5   Turn left at the signpost along White Lane; continue over the metal barrier on the stone chip surface and the grassy track to the road.

6   Turn right and follow the road; just before the chevrons for the right hand bend turn left at the sign down the right hand side of the field. Cross a stile and a footbridge keeping direction next to the stream. Bear right over a stile and regain direction left next to a wire fence. Bear right over the next stile and left along the left hand field edge; continue across two stiles to a junction of paths.

7   Take the path to the left with the wire link fence and the lake on the left up to the road, turn right and walk 300yds to the green hoop barrier on the left. Go into the country park and follow the path to the right, through the trees and parallel to the road back to the car park and your vehicle.

15

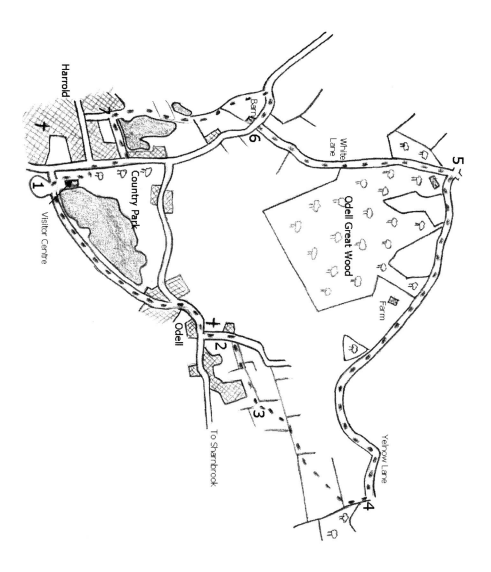

Harrold

Barn

White Lane

5

6

Country Park

Visitor Centre

1

Odell Great Wood

Farm

Odell

2

3

To Sharnbrook

Yellow Lane

4

S:E

4 Bromham Mill

$6^3/_4$ Miles   3 Hours

Park in the car park at the crossroads at Kempston Church End off the A5134 between Bromham and Kempston. No facilities.

1 Turn left at the entrance and follow the track through the trees parallel to the road. Bear right down the walled road past the school and through the kissing gate. Continue on the gravel path between trees.

2 Pass through the barriers and walk past the houses, bearing left. Turn right then immediate left past the no cycling signs along the fenced path and the road beyond. Bear left into Riverview Way, go up to the footpath sign (to Biddenham), turn left and follow the road right.

3 Cross both footbridges and continue ahead on the right hand field edge with the hedge and the dyke on the right, just after the hedge on the left starts turn left at a junction of paths.

4 Keep direction along the track over the golf course and past the backs of the houses, bear right to some metal gates; turn left just in front of them and follow the hedge. Turn right at the metal gate and go down the concrete path to the road, turn left, walk to the end and turn right between the church and Church Barn.

5 Carefully cross over the A428 and turn left at the next road (the old A428). Go over narrow Bromham Bridge and walk past the watermill entrance. Continue to the T-junction by the supermarket and turn left down signposted Thistley Lane.

6 Fork right at the marker post, go between the trees back to the A428 and cross, bear right up the ramp and follow the arrowed direction over the field to the corner of Hanger Wood, continue along the side of the wood to a marker post.

7 Turn left and walk upslope with the hedge to the right, keep direction from the yellow topped marker post over the field which may be under cultivation; carry on through the hedge gap to the road and turn right. Turn left after 400yds over the stile and cross to the opposite corner, step over this stile and continue to the road with the hedge and the dyke to the right.

8 Turn left for just over a quarter of a mile to the signpost, turn right over the sleeper bridge and cross the field on what should be an obvious track; continue past the cemetery to the road. Turn left and walk down to find your vehicle in the car park on the other side of the crossroads.

15

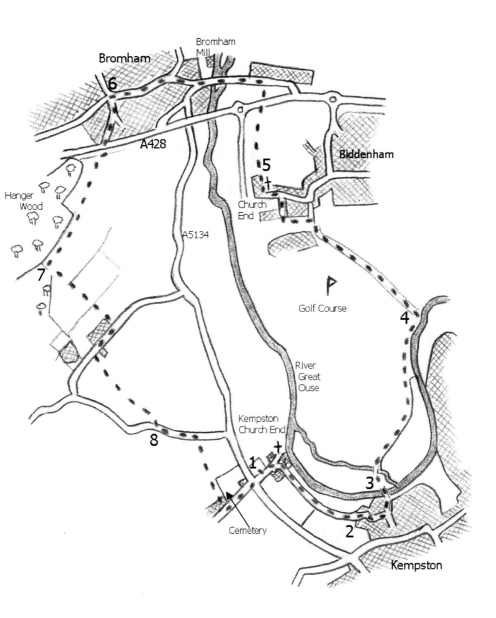

Bromham

Bromham Mill

6

A428

Hanger Wood

7

A5134

5

Church End

Biddenham

Golf Course

4

River Great Ouse

8

Kempston Church End

1

Cemetery

3

2

Kempston

5   St Nicholas's Church

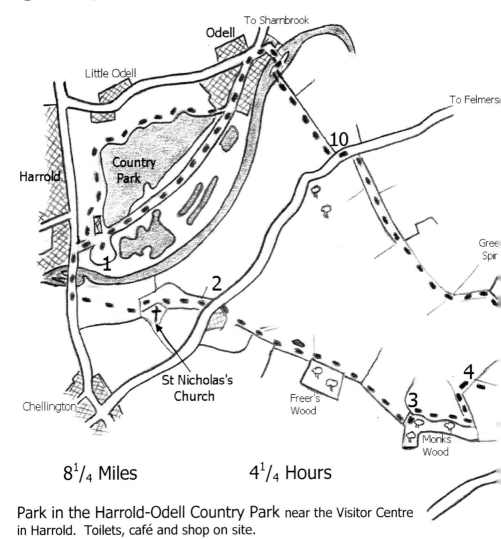

8¹/₄ Miles   **4¹/₄ Hours**

Park in the Harrold-Odell Country Park near the Visitor Centre in Harrold. Toilets, café and shop on site.

1   Go back out from the car park to the road and turn left; cross the narrow bridge over the Great Ouse. On the other side fork left down a slope to a footpath sign on the left. Go over the stile and cross the field to the corner by the church. Carry on past St Nicholas's Church (which is now a private residential centre) to the top left corner; cross the stile and the road.

2   Follow the signposted direction and cross the stile at the corner of the barn. Go along the right hand field edge, through the gate and continue direction on the field edge past the yellow topped post. Keep going over two stiles and past Freer's Wood, go through the hedge gap by the marker post and down the right hand field edge. Walk a short way into Monks Wood, turn left at a marker post go through the gate ahead and turn right.

3   Carry on down the field edge, turn left along the farm road, walk up the slope with the hedge to the right and follow to the right through a gateway.

4   After 75yds turn right through a gateway and go down the left hand field edge. At the hedge turn right for 40yds, cross the stile and keep direction over a stile/footbridge and the field beyond (a track should be visible through any crop) to the corner. Cross this stile and go diagonally left over the field, keep direction through a narrow gate to the stile in the bottom corner. Cross and follow the path along the backs of the houses to a yellow topped marker post by a white cottage.

5   Bear right down the stone path to the road in Pavenham and turn left along the roadside path out of the village.

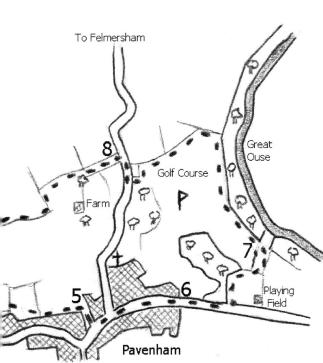

To Felmersham

Great Ouse

Golf Course

Farm

Playing Field

Pavenham

6   Just past the golf club entrance turn left at the signpost and follow the left hand edge of the playing fields to the tennis nets at the top right. Go through the kissing gate and follow the obvious track to the next marker post.

7   Bear left and keep on the path between the river and the golf course. After half a mile, turn left uphill with the dyke to the right; bear left at the marker post still uphill with the dyke on the right to the hedge. Go left for 50yds then turn right to the road. Turn right along the road up to the bridleway sign on the left.

Completed on the next page (Fourteen)

15:E

8 Turn left and follow the track between fields past a small stand of trees to the hedge parallel with the telegraph poles. Turn left then right at the next marker post along the path between fields with the dyke to the left. Turn right in front of the narrow gate and walk up to Green's Spinney.

9 Turn left then right around the spinney, as the trees end bear left and then right at the marker post. Keeping to the right hand edges of the fields, go through the hedge gap and maintain direction towards Odell church in the middle distance. Follow the track past the yellow topped marker post to the road.

10 Go to the left down the road for 100yds and then right at the bridleway sign, continue down the right hand field edge to the bridge, cross and bear right. Turn left past the old mill and bear left along the road into Odell. Walk to the left of the 'Bell' along Horsefair Lane.

11 Go through the gate and keep direction on the gravel path to the car park and your vehicle (the path to the right from the gate leads around the other side of the lake past the visitor centre and back to the car park).

6 Piper's Highway

$6^3/_4$ Miles $3^1/_2$ Hours

Find a parking space in Stevington village, local pubs the 'Royal George' and the 'Red Lion'. No toilets.

1 Start from the crossroads by the village cross, walk towards Pavenham along Court Lane. Turn left after 200yds down the signposted footpath; continue with the dyke on the left into the field and into the left hand corner. Turn right uphill and bear right on the track over the field. Cross the stile ahead and follow the right hand field edge to the road, turn left and walk for 300yds up to the bridleway sign.

2 Go through the gate and along the right hand field edge, continue through the first small gate and turn right through the next gate just before the corner. Regain direction with the dyke to the left. At the top go through the hedge gap and turn right along the right hand field edge.

Completion on the next Page (Sixteen)

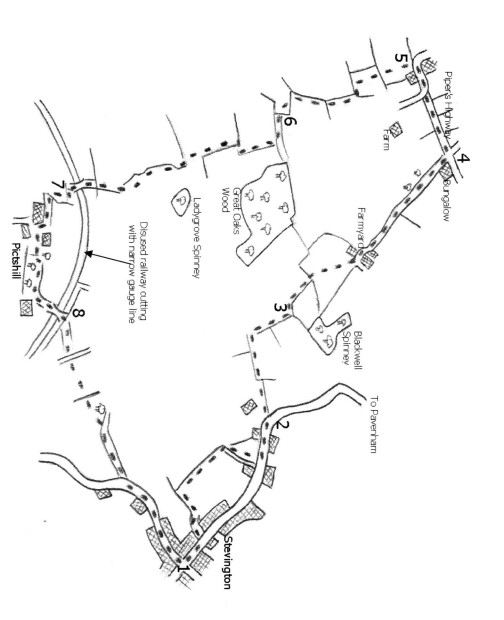

Piper's Highway

5

Farm

4

Bungalow

Farmyard

6

Great Oaks Wood

Ladygrove Spinney

Disused railway cutting with narrow gauge line

7

Pictshill

8

3

Blackwell Spinney

To Pavenham

2

Stevington

1

Completion of **6** Piper's Highway from previous page

3   At the marker post turn left to the hedge end, then right down the field edge with the hedge to the right. Carry on through the narrow gate and take a right hand diagonal to New Barns Farmyard at the top right. Go through the narrow metal gate and follow the concrete road between the farm buildings. Continue on the hardcore farm road down the slope to a crossroads next to a bungalow.

4   Turn left along the grass bridleway called Piper's Highway, which leads onto a tarmac road between cottages.

5   As this road turns right go left through a gate and follow the stony double track bridleway. Carry on through the next gateway over the field to the hedge and turn left. Turn right through the small gate and follow the farm track. At a marker post at the bottom of a slope take a left hand diagonal over the field corner, a path should be visible if there is a crop in this field, to another marker post and bear left.

6   Walk along the hedged path and turn right over a sleeper bridge before the wood. Carry on down the left hand field edge past the marker post with the trees and the hedge to the left. Go right for 50yds after the next hedge gap, go through the gate and follow the hedge. Keep direction past a narrow metal gate and past the pond to a wider metal gate marked by discs; go through and continue on the right hand side of this field. Turn right through the next marked metal gate along the obvious path on the left hand field edge with the hedge and the dyke to the left and carry on to the bridge over the disused railway line.

7   Cross and turn left through the high, wide gate, at the bottom of the slope turn right and cross the field and turn left through another high, wide gate. Follow the track with the fence to the left, keep direction on the grass through the next lower gate and turn right through the gateway at the marker post. Go through the hedge gap and turn left, bear right past the front of the house and continue ahead between hedges. Bear left after the first pond then right to regain direction and follow the track left. Cross the stile and the field beyond to the railway bridge.

8   Go through the narrow gate on the other side of the track passing the bridge and take a right hand diagonal along an obvious track. Cross over the gated pathway and continue ahead over the field. Pass the marker post and carry on along the left hand field edge and down the tree lined path. At the road turn left and walk into Stevington and your vehicle.

7   Pinchmill Islands

6 Miles   3 Hours

Find a parking space in Sharnbrook, pubs and shops in village, no toilets.

1   Walk along Park Lane from the corner with High Street. Turn right at the signpost through the cottage garden; go over the stile and take a left hand diagonal to the field corner. Follow the narrow path between fences and hedges to the footbridge/stile and cross. Turn right, go through the gateway and bear left.

2   Cross the stile furthest away from the hedge and go over the field on a slight right hand diagonal, a track should be visible within any crop, to the top corner. Walk past the signpost and over the stile; continue along the left hand field edge and across the railway bridge.

3   Carry on ahead between the fence and the hedge, maintain direction over several stiles and across both lanes of the A6, be careful this is a very busy road! Go up the steps and bear left along the track then right to walk parallel to the hedge. Follow the field edge right then left alongside the wood past two yellow topped marker posts, almost to the derelict farm buildings.

4   Turn right at the marker post, down the right hand edge of the left hand field and keep direction with the hedge on the right, to the road. Carry on along the road ahead, go straight on at the junction into Bourne End and pass the farm.

5   Turn right at the bridleway sign along the hardcore track, turn left at the marker post and bear right at the next yellow top marker post. Continue past Vicarage Farm and the bungalow to the A6 and cross. Step over the stile and bear left towards Stoke Mill, the large building ahead and cross the road.

Completion of instructions and map on the next page (Eighteen)

Completion of 7 Pinchmill Islands from previous page

6   Go down the road to the right of the mill, bear left then right over the iron railed footbridge. Keep direction along the fenced track and the hardcore then tarmac road uphill. Cross the railway bridge and go straight on at the T-junction.

7   At the signpost by the metal gates turn right; follow this track to a marker post and then turn left over the stile. Go down the right hand field edge and around the corner to cross a stile/footbridge; continue downhill and over another stile. Cross the stile in the next corner and bear immediate right over the adjacent stile. Turn left and keep direction between the hedge and the wire fence, bear left at the end over a stile/footbridge close to the river at Pinchmill Islands.

8   Cross to the right over the first footbridge, bear immediate right over the second footbridge; follow the path and go left over the third and fourth footbridge. Keep on the track to the fifth, wider sleeper footbridge; turn left then bear right over the sixth and final footbridge.

9   Take a right hand diagonal across the field on what should be an obvious path through any crop, to the gate, go through and follow the path past the windmill tower to the road. Turn left along High street to the corner of Park Lane.

Also by Clive Brown:-

'Easy Walking in South Bedfordshire and the North Chilterns'

Published by the Book Castle @ £8-99
37 walks in your favourite style

e-mail walkingcloseto@yahoo.co.uk for the best price

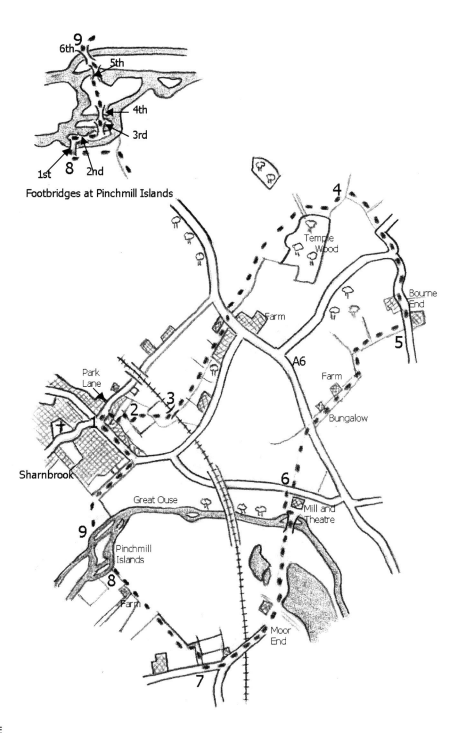

9
6th 5th
4th
3rd
1st 8 2nd

Footbridges at Pinchmill Islands

4

Temple Wood

Bourne End

Farm

A6 5

Farm

Bungalow

Park Lane

3

2

1

Sharnbrook

6

Great Ouse

Mill and Theatre

9

Pinchmill Islands

8

Farm

Moor End

7

8 Ravensden Brook

6 Miles $2^1/_2$ Hours

Park in the main car park of Mowsbury Park, off Wentworth Drive, toilets, refreshments (seasonal) and children's play area. An optional nature trail leads from the last part of the walk around Putnoe Wood.

1 Start along the path between the toilets and the play area away from Wentworth Drive. Follow the path left along the backs of the houses to Kimbolton Road. Cross by the traffic lights and turn right to follow the signed bridleway between the hedge and the fence. Turn left at the end, still parallel with but further away from the houses, bear left at the corner, cross the footbridge and turn right.

2 Follow the right hand field edge, turn right then left, to regain direction at a yellow topped marker post. Continue and turn right at the next (first) marker post and climb the hill with the corrugated iron barn and the hedge to the left.

3 At the road go slight right, cross the sleeper footbridge, go through the kissing gate and continue over the field on a very slight left hand diagonal to the signpost standing in the middle of the field. Turn left and walk to the yellow top marker post which may be seen against the hedge corner; continue with the hedge on the right through the kissing gate and over footbridges to the road; turn right.

4 At the T-junction go down the cul-de-sac opposite; bear right then left between tall hedges. Take a right at a junction of farm roads, go to the corner where the road turns left in front of a horse jump; bear right down a narrow path and across two stiles close together. Turn left and walk parallel with Ravensden Brook.

5 Cross over the B660, keep direction through the scrapyard and along the field edge to the next road. Carry on through the trees of The Plantation and alongside the brook to a bridge between fields; cross and double back on the other side of the brook. Turn left at the marker post in the corner to walk between fields to the road.

6 Turn left along the roadside path for 200yds and turn right at the bridleway sign; keep going now on this well marked track, past Marsh Wood, the golf course and Putnoe Wood. Turn right at the road and follow the parallel tarmac bridleway back to the car park and your vehicle.

15:8

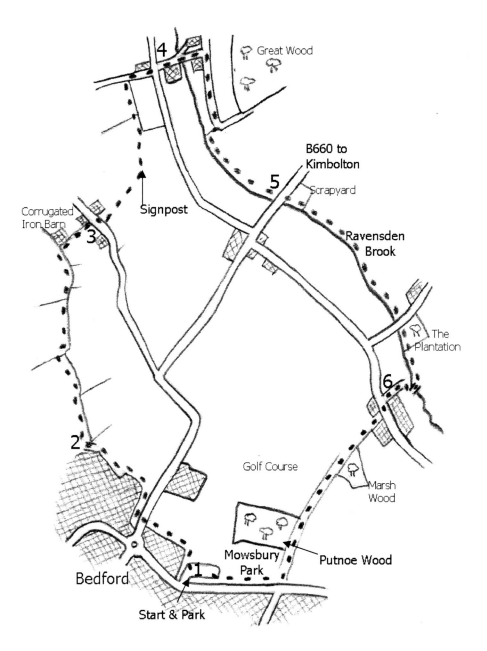

Great Wood

4

B660 to
Kimbolton

5

Scrapyard

Signpost

Corrugated
Iron Barn

3

Ravensden
Brook

The
Plantation

6

2

Golf Course

Marsh
Wood

Putnoe Wood

Mowsbury
Park

Bedford

1

Start & Park

5:E

9   Hanger Wood

5³/₄ Miles   2³/₄ Hours

Find a parking space in Bromham village. No toilets.

1   Start from the corner of Northampton Road and Stagsden Road in front of the supermarket. Go along Northampton Road; turn left before the next corner down the tarmac road past the footpath sign to Stagsden. Continue past the houses, through the gate ahead and along the left hand field edge. Go through the next gate and change to the right hand field edge at the marker post. Keep going to the marker post in the corner by the A428, turn left and go through the gate.

2   Cross this busy road carefully and follow the signposted direction over the field corner and continue along the edge; bear right in the corner, left at the marker post and keep direction past the end of White's Wood. Walk through the wide gap and turn left with the wood still on the left to the corner and turn right. Go left through the gap at the marker post and bear right along the edge of the lawn next to the conifers, continue through the gate and turn right down the tarmac track.

3   Bear left and keep direction on the grass path and the right hand field edge, all the way to the road.

4   Keep straight on, over the field on a track which may be under cultivation but should be visible within any crop; continue through another gap and down the slope (track again should be well marked) to a metal gate and go through.

5   Turn left, down the left hand field edge and over the stile; go over the narrow neck of field ahead to the farm road. Turn left along the road to the junction and bear left into Stagsden, to the junction just past the church.

6   Take the road left and follow the road left to the signpost on the right, descend the steps and keep direction to the A422.

7   Cross carefully and carry on over the concrete bridge, bear left at the marker post up the hill through the golf course. Bear right past the wood, Oxleys; at the marker post at the corner turn left to the corner of Hanger Wood, turn right to walk with the wood to the left and go up the path through the trees.

8   Bear left with the path, along the edge of the wood and keep on the track and down the ramp back to the A428. Cross carefully and keep ahead along the bridleway bearing left into Bromham village and your vehicle.

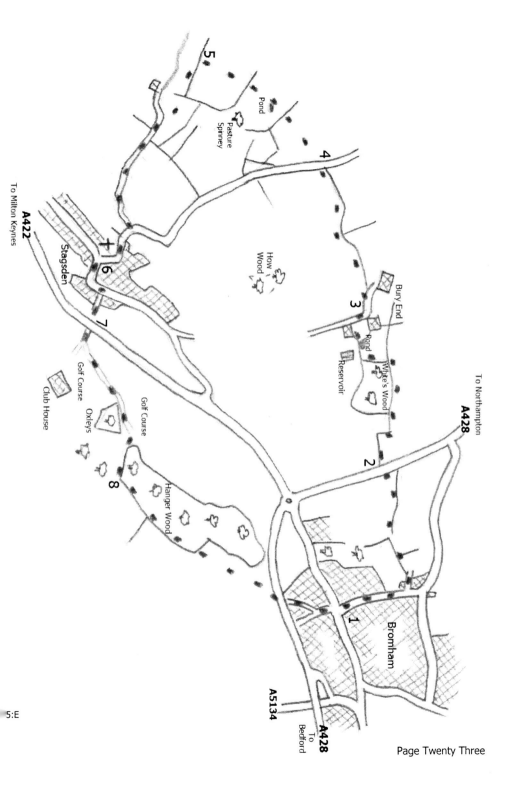

The 'Walking Close to' Series

<u>South and South West</u>

Chichester and the South Downs (2015)
The New Forest (North and West)
Romsey and the Test Valley
Cheddar Gorge
Exmouth and East Devon
Corsham and Box (Wiltshire)
The Quantock Hills (West Somerset)
Blandford Forum (Dorset)
Salisbury (2015)

Winchester (2015)
The New Forest (South and East)
The East Devon Coast
Glastonbury and the City of Wells
The Avon near Bath
The Avon near Chippenham (Wiltshire)
Shaftesbury (Dorset)
Bradford-on-Avon (Wiltshire)

<u>East Anglia and Lincolnshire</u>

The Nene near Peterborough
Lavenham (Suffolk)
The Nene Valley Railway near Wansford
The Nene near Oundle
The Great North Road near Stilton
Bury St Edmunds
Norfolk Broads (Northern Area)
Southwold and the Suffolk Coast
North West Norfolk (Hunstanton and Wells)
North Norfolk (Cromer and Sheringham)
The Lincolnshire Wolds (North)
The Stour near Sudbury (Suffolk)
Chelmsford
Epping Forest (Essex/North London)
The Colne near Colchester
Thetford Forest (Norfolk/Suffolk)
The Great Ouse in Huntingdonshire
The Torpel Way (Stamford to Peterborough)

Grafham Water (Huntingdonshire)
Dedham Vale (Suffolk/Essex)
The Cam and the Granta near Cambridge
Lincoln
The Welland near Stamford
The Isle of Ely
Norfolk Broads (Southern Area)
Aldeburgh, Snape and Thorpeness
Clare, Cavendish and Haverhill
Bourne and the Deepings
The Lincolnshire Wolds (South)
The Orwell near Ipswich
Stowmarket (Suffolk)
Hertford and the Lee Valley
Newmarket
The Great Ouse near King's Lynn
South Lincolnshire

<u>Midlands</u>

The Nene near Thrapston
The Nene near Wellingborough
The River Ise near Kettering
The Nene near Northampton
Rockingham Forest (Northamptonshire)
Daventry and North West Northamptonshire
Rugby
Stratford-upon-Avon
Rutland Water
Eye Brook near Uppingham
The Soar near Leicester
Lutterworth (Leicestershire)
The Vale of Belvoir (North Leicestershire)
Melton Mowbray
The Welland near Market Harborough
Banbury
South West Herefordshire

The Great Ouse near Bedford
Woburn Abbey (Bedfordshire)
Sherwood Forest
Pitsford Water (Northamptonshire)
The Thames near Oxford
The Trent near Nottingham
The Vale of White Horse
Henley-on-Thames
The River Pang (Reading/Newbury)
The Great Ouse north of Milton Keynes
The Cotswolds near Witney
The Malvern Hills
The Dukeries (Sherwood Forest)
The Severn near Worcester
Woodstock and Blenheim Palace
The Kennet near Newbury

<u>Cumbria</u>
Cartmel and Southern Lakeland

<u>Cheshire</u>
Chester and Delamere Forest (2015

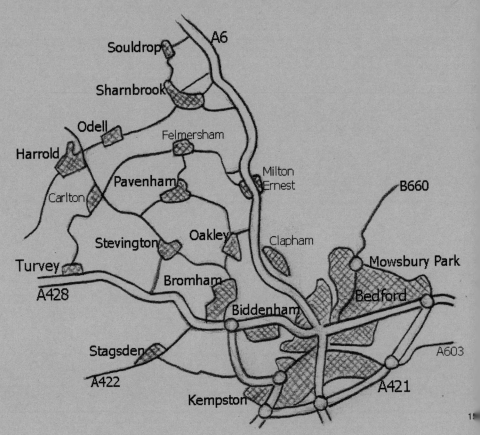

**We hope you have enjoyed these walks
there are over 80 titles in the 'Walking Close to' series
Look out for**

Walking Close To
The Nene near Northampton
The Great Ouse north of Milton Keynes
The Great Ouse in Huntingdonshire
Woburn Abbey (Bedfordshire)
The Cam and the Granta near Cambridge
The Great North Road near Stilton
The Isle of Ely
The Nene near Wellingborough
Grafham Water
Rutland Water

£3.25

ISBN 978-1-907669-15-6

9 781907 669156